DESERT FOX
SEIF
BIN ZIYAZAN

Retold by Denys Johnson-Davies
Illustrations by Gameel Shafeek

HOOPOE BOOKS

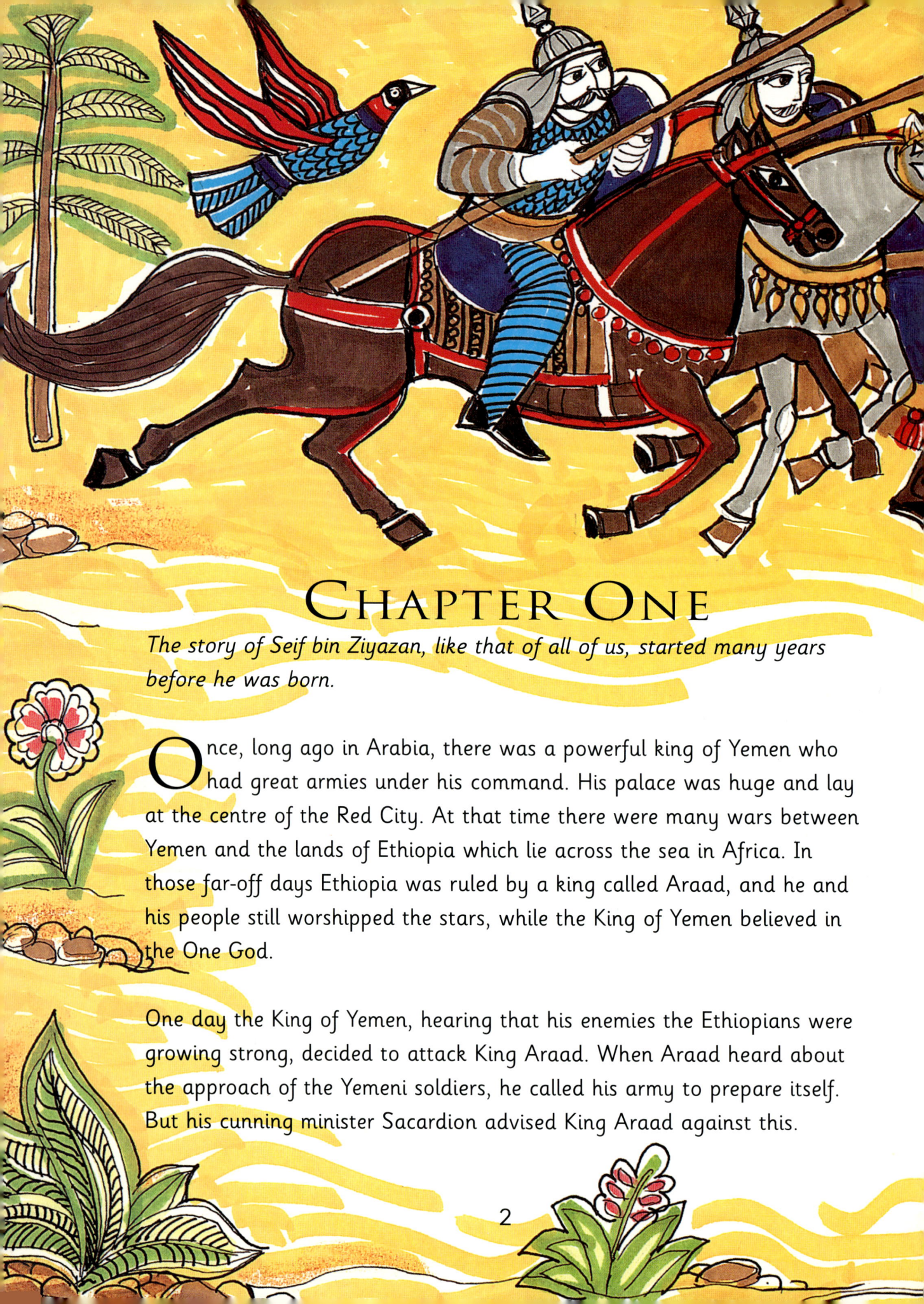

CHAPTER ONE

The story of Seif bin Ziyazan, like that of all of us, started many years before he was born.

Once, long ago in Arabia, there was a powerful king of Yemen who had great armies under his command. His palace was huge and lay at the centre of the Red City. At that time there were many wars between Yemen and the lands of Ethiopia which lie across the sea in Africa. In those far-off days Ethiopia was ruled by a king called Araad, and he and his people still worshipped the stars, while the King of Yemen believed in the One God.

One day the King of Yemen, hearing that his enemies the Ethiopians were growing strong, decided to attack King Araad. When Araad heard about the approach of the Yemeni soldiers, he called his army to prepare itself. But his cunning minister Sacardion advised King Araad against this.

"The Arab armies are powerful and we cannot be certain of defeating them in battle. Instead, mighty king, I have thought of an idea which will make it unnecessary to fight them."

So King Araad and his minister Sacardion chose a beautiful slave-girl called Kamariyya and sent her as a gift to the King of Yemen. But even as a young girl Kamariyya was known for her cruelty: it was as though she had been born without a heart. The minister gave her a bottle of poison and told her she would be well rewarded if she succeeded in killing the Yemeni king.

As soon as he saw her, the King of Yemen fell in love with Kamariyya and married her and made her his queen. After this, Kamariyya was able to carry out her wicked orders to kill the king. She did this by giving him small amounts of poison for many days so that he became weaker and weaker, without knowing the reason. At the same time, Kamariyya found that she was going to have the king's child.

When the king was near death he made his will and declared that Kamariyya, his wife and queen, should continue to rule until she had had her child. If the child was a boy, then he would become king and rule the Red City.

Everyone was happy when, just after the king's death, Kamariyya gave birth to a boy, who was named Seif bin Ziyazan. But the queen herself felt only hatred for her son from the moment he was born. This was because she knew that one day he would rule over the Red City instead of her. Kamariyya was greedy for power and was unable to accept that her own child should rule in her place. She therefore began to plan for the little baby's death in the same way as she had planned the death of his father.

Kamariyya realised that if she herself killed the baby someone might find out; the people would rise against her and put her to death for her crime. She therefore decided to speak to one of her maidservants.

"If you do not help me to kill this child," Kamariyya told the maidservant, "I shall say that I rescued the child when you were about to strangle him in his cradle - and you know what your fate will be then!"

The maidservant was horrified at the thought that the young baby would be killed, but she was too frightened of Kamariyya to refuse. She suggested to her mistress that they should take the baby to a desert known as the Valley of Death and that they should leave him there.

"If he lives, he lives; and if he dies, he dies. It will not be either of us that kills him, but I do not see how he will escape death in that desert full of lions and wild beasts."

So Kamariyya and the maidservant rode for three whole days and nights until they reached the Valley of Death. There, under a thorn bush, they left the helpless baby.

Kamariyya had planned that as soon as they arrived back at the Red City she would kill her maidservant, to make sure that no-one could ever discover what had happened to the baby. The maidservant, however, guessed what was in Kamariyya's mind; so one night, as they were riding in the darkness, she suddenly galloped away on her horse to a nearby oasis where some of her relatives had tents. From then on she lived the life of a nomad and never returned to the Red City.

In the desert where the two women had left the baby, there lived a gazelle. She herself had a baby which was feeding from her milk. One day the gazelle became frightened at the approach of a hunter. She ran away, hoping to return later and find her baby gazelle; but when she returned the baby gazelle was no longer there. As she searched in the surrounding desert, the gazelle heard the crying of the baby boy under a thorn bush. Since she no longer had a child of her own, the gazelle lay down by the human child and fed him from her milk. In this way the baby was saved.

Later, the same hunter passed by and saw with amazement the gazelle giving her milk to the baby. The hunter allowed the gazelle to escape, took the baby in his arms and carried him to his home which was in the city of Dour. This city lay in the lands ruled by Araad, king of the Ethiopians - although the city itself was ruled by Prince Afrah who, like King Araad himself, worshipped the stars.

The following day the hunter carried the baby to the palace and explained to Prince Afrah how he had found him under a thorn bush. As the prince took the child from the hunter, the child gave the prince a smile that won his heart; from then on, Prince Afrah loved the baby as though it was his own child.

At that moment shouts were heard and a servant entered and announced that Sacardion, the minister of Araad, king of all the Ethiopians, was making his way to the palace. He had come in order to receive from Prince Afrah the taxes that were owed by the city of Dour.

As the minister entered, Prince Afrah rose to his feet to greet him. It was this same Sacardion who had sent Queen Kamariyya to kill the baby's father.

When he saw the baby, Sacardion asked about him. Prince Afrah told Sacardion how a hunter had found him in the desert. Sacardion lifted up the child but hatred entered his heart when he noticed a birthmark on the side of the baby's face.

"This child must be killed," he said.

"But why?" asked Prince Afrah. "We have decided to bring him up in the palace."

"Have you not noticed the birthmark on his cheek?" asked Sacardion. "It is a warning to us who worship the stars. In the ancient books it is written that a boy will appear called Seif bin Ziyazan with this mark on his cheek, and that he will overcome our gods."

While they were talking, a messenger hurried in to announce to Prince Afrah that his wife had just given birth to a daughter. Prince Afrah immediately went to his wife. As he looked at his child, he saw that she too - like the baby boy who had been found in the desert - had a

birthmark on her cheek. He carried her back to where he had been sitting and placed his daughter beside the boy child.

"I do not think it is just a coincidence that these two babies have the same birthmark," he said, and then and there he named his daughter Shama, which in Arabic means "birthmark".

The minister Sacardion was filled with anger at the sight of the two babies lying side by side. "If these two birthmarks come together," he hissed, "it will be the end of our worship of the stars. The two of them would bring disaster upon us. It would mean that the kingdom of the Ethiopians will finish and will be replaced by the rule of the Arabs. Both the girl and the boy must therefore be put to death!"

Prince Afrah was furious: "Are you asking me to kill my own daughter?" he asked. "Are you mad? And the boy, what has he done wrong?"

Although he was so angry, Prince Afrah had to remember that Sacardion was the minister of the powerful King Araad, and that his own city of Dour was part of Araad's kingdom.

"As from today," Prince Afrah said to Sacardion, "I agree that the two babies will be separated. Neither of them will know about the other."

Then Prince Afrah named the boy "Desert Fox" because he had been discovered in the wild emptiness of the desert. Of course, neither Prince Afrah nor anyone else knew that the baby's real name was Seif bin Ziyazan and that his father had been the King of Yemen, the great enemy of the Ethiopians.

CHAPTER TWO

The baby boy was looked after by a nurse. One day, as the nurse was filling a jar with drinking-water, she heard a strange voice calling to her: "Prepare Desert Fox for going away. He will be brought up with me until he is three years old."

The nurse was frightened by this voice from nowhere and realised that it was a genie speaking. She therefore made the child ready and left him beside the water jar. She turned her back and when she looked again, the child had disappeared. The nurse reported to Prince Afrah what had happened. As she had worked for many years at the palace, the prince believed her story. Although he was sad, he told himself that no doubt the genie that had taken Desert Fox would return him again.

Prince Afrah and everyone at the palace missed the young boy and waited impatiently for his return. Then, one morning, as he was leaving his palace, the prince heard a voice calling to him: "Prince Afrah, be happy; the child, Desert Fox, will now be returned to you. Look after him well, for he is the son of a great king and one day he will be a great king himself. Bring him up so that he may play his part in the world."

"And who are you?" asked Prince Afrah, trembling with fear.

The voice answered: "I am the Queen of the Mountains of the Moon and the sources of the Nile. I am the wife of the White King of the Genies. A human cannot, after a certain age, continue to live with genies, so I am now giving the boy back to you."

Prince Afrah looked down and saw that Desert Fox was standing by his side. He was full of joy at having the young boy back at the palace, and he brought the very best teachers to teach him how to ride, how to fight with the sword and the spear, and how to shoot with a bow and arrow. Soon Desert Fox became the most skilled of all the young men in the palace, in spite of his young age. As Desert Fox grew stronger day by day, the champion of the other young men saw that he would soon challenge him. Desert Fox felt that his life was in danger from this man and his friends, who all envied the way Prince Afrah treated him. So early one morning he untied his horse and rode into the safety of the open desert.

For two whole days and nights he travelled. On the morning of the third day he saw a cave in the distance. He rode up to the opening and as he stood there, he heard a human voice. Desert Fox was frightened at the idea of a human being living in such a wild place. What sort of person could this be? But hunger and thirst led Desert Fox into the cave.

Sitting inside the cave was a man from a foreign land, who greeted him with the words: "My son, I have been waiting for you for a long time. There is a magic whip here which can only be taken by a young man whose name is Desert Fox. I know that you are this Desert Fox, so go to the back of the cave and bring out the magic whip."

"And what is the magic of this whip?" asked Desert Fox.

The man said: "It is written that you will soon have to face a powerful giant. No weapon is of any use against this giant, except this magic whip." Desert Fox went to the back of the cave where he came to a low bed on which lay a very old man with a white beard. Under the man's head Desert Fox saw a short leather whip with a golden handle. He reached out to take hold of it and at that moment the eyes of the old man opened wide and looked at him.

"Welcome, Desert Fox," the old man said in a trembling voice. "I remember you from the time when you were living with the Queen of the Mountains of the Moon. Take the whip and may its magic protect you from the giant. Remember, though, that once you have used it the whip will return by itself to me."

Then the old man closed his eyes again and Desert Fox took the whip from under his head. At the opening to the cave the man from a foreign land stood waiting for him, holding his horse by the reins. Desert Fox got on his horse and again set off into the desert. After a long and tiring journey, he found himself in front of the high walls of a great city. Its gates were locked against him and its people were gathered on the walls. They were all crying and shouting as though someone whom they loved had just died.

By one of the city gates, Desert Fox found a large tent. From the way it was decorated he knew that a bride was waiting inside. When he approached the tent and looked inside, Desert Fox saw a young girl of great beauty sitting on her own and crying. How was it, he asked himself, that everyone was crying when there was going to be a wedding?

"What are you crying for?" he asked the girl.

"Young stranger," she answered through her tears, "I am the daughter of a prince, but my father has been forced to marry me to a terrible giant."

14

As she lifted her head, Desert Fox saw the birthmark on her cheek, exactly like the one he had.

"How could such a thing happen?" he asked.

She wiped away the tears from her eyes before replying: "My name is Shama and I am the daughter of Prince Afrah, ruler of the city of Dour. A wicked man called Sacardion has always hated my father because he refused to put me to death at the time of my birth. So he arranged for a terrible giant to come and destroy our city. The giant attacked us with lightning and thunder and in the end my father, Prince Afrah, had to agree to give me to the giant to save the city from destruction."

"So you are Shama, daughter of Prince Afrah!" exclaimed Desert Fox. He was going to tell her about himself when the side of the tent was torn open with a blinding flash of light, and there, standing in front of them, was the giant. He had come to take Shama away. His angry face had a single eye in the middle of the forehead. The long arms, covered in black hair, ended in sharp claws that were now pointing at Desert Fox.

Desert Fox quickly took out his whip. The giant looked at it and laughed. Desert Fox wondered how he could fight the giant with such a small whip, but he lifted it in the air and brought it down across the giant's arm.

The giant screamed with pain as the whip cut completely through his arm. Quickly he bent down and picked up the arm with his other hand and placed it where it had been cut off. He was afraid that the smoke which filled his body instead of blood would come out and he would die. Then, still screaming, the giant made his escape and Desert Fox found that the whip was no longer in his hand.

CHAPTER THREE

Alone once more, Desert Fox told Shama about himself and how he had spent his childhood at her father's palace.

"Then how was it that we never met?" asked Shama, who was amazed by this handsome young man who had rescued her from the giant.

"I believe that your father kept us apart on purpose," said Desert Fox.

"Why would he do that?" demanded Shama.

Desert Fox was silent for a while as he thought about Shama's question.

"Perhaps there was someone who did not want us to meet," he answered. They went on talking and soon Desert Fox knew that he loved Shama, so he told her that he would like her to be his wife.

"Then go and ask my father!" said Shama.

At the palace Prince Afrah welcomed Desert Fox like a long-lost son. But when Desert Fox told him how he had rescued Shama from the giant and that he now wanted to marry her, Prince Afrah said that he would have to consult Sacardion, the minister of King Araad.

Sacardion had always feared that these two young people might one day meet. He knew that this would mean the end of the worship of the stars and of the greatness of the Ethiopians. Sacardion told Prince Afrah, "As the price of your daughter's hand in marriage, demand that this man brings you the head of the famous warrior Saadoun the Black."

Sacardion knew that no-one had ever defeated Saadoun in battle and that he would certainly kill Desert Fox.

Desert Fox was determined to win Shama for his wife and to bring the head of Saadoun the Black to Prince Afrah. He therefore set off once again into the desert to make the long journey to the fort where Saadoun lived.

When Desert Fox arrived at the fort he found no-one guarding the main gate. The gate was partly open and Desert Fox could see eighty powerful men, all standing in lines in an open space. At the side was a tall figure, dressed in armour, with a handsome black face, sharp eyes and a neat moustache and beard. Desert Fox knew at once that this man must be the warrior Saadoun.

Saadoun was watching two of his men fighting with long sticks. He was shouting advice to them and Desert Fox realised that Saadoun and his men were training in man-to-man combat.

Desert Fox moved and his foot slipped on a stone which made a noise as it rolled away. Saadoun sent one of his men to see what had happened, but as soon as the man came through the gate Desert Fox struck him with his sword. Then Saadoun sent a second man and the same thing happened. So Saadoun decided to go himself, and soon he and Desert Fox were fighting a battle to the death. Sometimes it seemed that Saadoun was winning because of his great strength; at other times, Desert Fox's skill with the sword gave him the advantage. Then, as they fought, Saadoun's sword suddenly slipped from his hand and he was at Desert Fox's mercy. But Desert Fox, instead of killing his enemy, bent down and picked up Saadoun's sword.

"I would not wish to kill someone who was defenceless," said Desert Fox, and he gave the sword to Saadoun.

"And I would not wish to kill an opponent as noble as yourself," answered Saadoun the Black.

Then Saadoun asked him why he had come to the fort, and Desert Fox told him how he had promised to bring Saadoun's head as the price for the hand of Shama.

"Then take me to Prince Afrah as your prisoner," suggested Saadoun. "After all, he did not say that my head had to be separated from my body!"

. . .

Prince Afrah was in his palace when a messenger entered and announced that some men were approaching. The evil Sacardion was sitting with Prince Afrah and they both recognised the tall figure of Saadoun.

Prince Afrah was frightened that Saadoun was coming to take revenge from the man who had demanded his head. When Saadoun, with Desert Fox, entered and refused to sit, Prince Afrah's heart trembled with fear.

"Could you think of no other price for your daughter's hand than my head?" shouted Saadoun angrily. "Without the noble generosity of Desert Fox, my head would have been brought to you cut off from my body."

Prince Afrah looked at Desert Fox and then at Sacardion, for he did not know how to reply to Saadoun. Sacardion saw that he and Prince Afrah were at the mercy of Desert Fox and Saadoun, so he pretended to be happy that both were alive and had become friends.

"Let us celebrate the good news that no blood has been spilt," said Sacardion. "Tomorrow Prince Afrah can decide about his daughter."

So the next morning Desert Fox went to see Prince Afrah to demand Shama's hand in marriage. But the wicked Sacardion had talked to the Prince and had reminded him of their agreement that Saadoun's head was to be the price.

Prince Afrah shook his head as he answered Desert Fox: "Desert Fox, you did not do what was asked of you. You did not bring me the head of Saadoun the Black. As the two of you have become friends, I shall not demand that of you. Instead, as the price of my daughter's hand, I now ask you to bring me the Book of the Nile. Then I swear by all the stars in the heavens that I shall give you my daughter Shama as your wife."

"And where is this Book of the Nile to be found?" asked Desert Fox.

"I do not know, my son. It is for you to find it and bring it to me. Only then will Shama be yours."

CHAPTER FOUR

Desert Fox said goodbye to the beautiful Shama and set off alone to search for the Book of the Nile. He felt that he had been cheated by Prince Afrah and the wicked Sacardion. Had he not defeated the great Saadoun in battle? Now he had another task to carry out before he could win Shama. But if the price for Shama was to be the Book of the Nile, then he would bring it to her father, even if he had to go to the ends of the world.

After sixty days and nights of wandering through deserts he saw in the distance a small hut on the side of a mountain. As he approached, he could hear a man's voice repeating the name of God and saying his prayers. Desert Fox called out a greeting. The voice was silent, then said:

"Welcome to you, Seif bin Ziyazan, future King of Yemen. Get down from your horse and let it rest after all these days of travelling."

"To whom are you talking, friend?" asked Desert Fox. "My name is Desert Fox and I am not a king."

"Desert Fox is the name Prince Afrah gave you," said the voice. "But your real name is Seif bin Ziyazan and it is written in the ancient books that you will bring victory to Islam against those who worship stars and idols. The time has now come for you to know your proper name."

When he had sat down in front of the holy man, whose name was Sheikh Jiyad, Desert Fox told him his story and how he had been asked to bring the Book of the Nile as the price for Shama's hand.

"No-one but God Almighty can help you to find this book," said Sheikh Jiyad. "As for now, you must eat something and have some sleep, for you have another tiring journey in front of you. It is a journey for which you will not need your horse, so leave it here outside my hut. Tomorrow we shall speak again and I shall tell you as much as I can about the journey you must make."

In the morning, Sheikh Jiyad described to Desert Fox how he must climb the mountain that lay opposite the hut, and how he must cross the mountain to the other side. There he would find a great area of water and one of the animals of the sea would be waiting to carry him to where he must go.

"And where is that?" asked Desert Fox eagerly.

"All will be revealed in its time," answered Sheikh Jiyad with a smile. "I have told you all I know."

Desert Fox thanked Sheikh Jiyad for his hospitality and slept the night in the hut. The next day he set off on his journey, crossing the mountain on foot until he found, as Sheikh Jiyad had told him, the sea animal by the water's edge. He climbed onto its back and it took him to the other side.

In his wanderings in search of the Book of the Nile, Desert Fox learned that in a certain city there were people who worshipped this book and looked on it as their god. The people and their king had special ways of discovering whether any stranger had entered the city to steal their book.

After crossing the sea on the back of the animal, Desert Fox saw in the distance a beautiful white city that shone in the sun. From the descriptions

he had heard he knew that this was the city he was looking for. Though Desert Fox succeeded in entering the city, he was quickly discovered. The guards of the city caught him, tied his hands and legs and threw him into a deep pit, where they were going to leave him to die of hunger.

As he lay at the bottom of the pit, without food or water, Desert Fox prayed to God to help him, for he saw no way of escaping. Suddenly, to his amazement, a great hole appeared in the wall of the pit, and through it flew a genie who called him by the name Seif bin Ziyazan and immediately untied the ropes that held his hands and feet.

"You cannot recognise me," said the genie, "for you were still a young child when you first knew me. I am the Queen of the Mountains of the Moon and you lived with me during the early years of your life. I have followed your story all this time. Until now you have had no need of me, but the time has come for me to help you. I know that there is nothing you want more in life than the Book of the Nile, for through it you will win the beautiful Shama. First, though, you must meet Sheikh Abdul Salam, a true man of God who has been our teacher."

The genie touched Desert Fox on his forehead and the two of them flew through the hole in the wall to a cave high up on a distant mountain.

"Enter," said the genie to Desert Fox, and then disappeared, though she promised him that she would again be at his service the next day.

Inside the cave Desert Fox found an old, white-haired man saying his prayers. When he had finished, he turned to Desert Fox and said: "I have something to give you and something to ask of you." He then took from inside his cloak the magic whip which had mysteriously been taken from his hand when he had used it against the giant.

"You will need this," said Sheikh Abdul Salam, handing the whip to Desert Fox. "Tomorrow the genie will take you to a castle. There you will meet people who are in great danger and it is only you and the magic whip that can rescue them."

"And what is it that you wish of me, holy Sheikh?" asked Desert Fox.

"That you return here with the genie after you have done what you have to do, and that you keep me company on my last night."

Desert Fox was about to say something, but the Sheikh interrupted: "Do not ask any questions. Do you agree to return here?"

"I agree," said Desert Fox.

The next morning the genie returned and took Desert Fox to a dark castle which appeared to have neither gates nor windows. He walked around its high walls but saw no way by which he could enter. Suddenly he noticed that a long rope was coming down from high above. He tied the rope around his body and was pulled upwards to the top of the wall. When he was inside the castle, Desert Fox found himself surrounded by forty young girls. They explained to him that they had been captured by a terrible giant and brought to this castle. They were all princesses from different parts of the world and they had been waiting for someone to come and rescue them.

Then, while he was talking to the girls, there was a crash of thunder and a blaze of lightning. A tall, one-eyed giant stood before them. Immediately Desert Fox recognised him as the same giant whose hand he had cut off. Now he knew why he needed the magic whip again. The giant stared in hatred at Desert Fox. But before the giant could move against him, Desert Fox brought out the whip. At the sight of it, the giant stepped back in terror. But Desert Fox had no mercy and hit out with the whip. At once the giant's body burst into flames and became a pile of ashes.

Though the girls were unable to see her, the genie once again stood before Desert Fox. He asked for each girl to be returned safely to her family. Then, with the genie's help, he was transported back to Sheikh Abdul Salam's hut.

"My time in this world is now over," the Sheikh told him. Desert Fox stayed with him through the night. Early in the morning the holy Sheikh died and Desert Fox buried him beside the cave in which he had lived all his life.

When the genie came to Desert Fox the next morning, she first asked him for the magic whip. "You will need it no longer," she said, "and it must stay in my care."

"But you will need this," she added, "if you are to complete your task and take the Book of the Nile to Prince Afrah."

She then handed to Desert Fox what looked like an ordinary cap, the sort of cap which men wear under their turbans. "This is a magic cap," she said, "and whoever puts it on becomes invisible. Only with its help will you be able to reach the Book of the Nile. I shall take you to the city where this book is worshipped, but it is you alone who must bring it away."

In the city people were coming and going, but Desert Fox was invisible to them. He heard them saying that it was the day for their king and his ministers to go and worship the Book of the Nile. Desert Fox waited till they had passed; he then joined them, still invisible under his cap.

Once they were all in the temple and the king and his ministers were bowing down in worship, Desert Fox stepped between them and quickly picked up the Book of the Nile. Before anyone realised what had happened, he walked out of one of the gates of the city. There he met the genie, the Queen of the Mountains of the Moon.

"I shall now take you to the hut where Sheikh Jiyad lives," she said. "Give me the cap, for you will have no more use for it. You will also have no more use for me, so may God be with you in your future journeys."

When they reached the cave the genie disappeared forever from his life. Sheikh Jiyad greeted him, then said: "So at last you will get your wish. Your horse is where you left it. As for me, I am going on the long journey, the journey that every human being must one day make. So do with me as you did with my friend Sheikh Abdul Salam."

Sheikh Jiyad died during the night. Desert Fox prayed before making a grave for him beside his hut. Then Desert Fox got on his horse and set off in the direction of the city where Shama was waiting for him so that he could give the Book of the Nile to her father and claim her in marriage.

CHAPTER FIVE

Saadoun the Black became worried when his friend Desert Fox was away for so long. He went to see Prince Afrah in his palace to ask if he had any news. He warned the Prince that if Desert Fox did not return he would take his revenge of those responsible for his death, and first among them would be the minister Sacardion.

When Saadoun had gone back in anger to the tents where he and his men were living outside the city, Prince Afrah called for Sacardion to come to him so as to ask his advice.

"Do not worry, O Prince," said Sacardion. "I do not believe that Desert Fox will return safely. However, I suggest that you arrange for Shama to marry the great King Araad. Once she is married to the King, Desert Fox can do nothing."

When he had convinced Prince Afrah to give his daughter to the great King of the Ethiopians, Sacardion went to see the King. He spoke to him of Shama's great beauty and convinced the King that she would make a good wife. The King therefore ordered his most powerful warrior, called Darbal, to go to Prince Afrah with a letter asking for her hand.

While Prince Afrah was sitting with Sacardion and the warrior Darbal, Saadoun the Black suddenly appeared with some of his men. Prince Afrah and Sacardion both stood up to greet him, though they could see that Saadoun was in an angry mood. Darbal, however, did not move from where he was sitting.

"Who is that dog that does not stand to greet me?" demanded Saadoun.

Darbal himself turned and answered Saadoun: "I am Darbal, messenger of the great Araad, King of the Ethiopians. He has sent me here to ask Prince Afrah for his daughter's hand in marriage."

Saadoun was shocked to hear this. "But she is promised to another," he protested.

"What other?" demanded Darbal, turning to Prince Afrah. But, as usual, Prince Afrah could find no answer. He therefore turned to the minister Sacardion, who answered Darbal:

"Shama is of course free to marry King Araad."

Saadoun went up to Darbal, who was still seated, and said to him: "What you are hearing is a lie. Go back to your master and tell him that Shama is promised to Desert Fox. Get up from your chair, dog, and tell your master the truth."

Darbal then got quickly to his feet, and the two men, both famous for their bravery and skill at fighting, began a battle in the middle of the palace hall. After a long fight, Saadoun succeeded in striking Darbal a blow that went right through his powerful body. Darbal fell to the ground, blood pouring from the wound. Seconds later, Darbal was dead and Saadoun made his escape.

Prince Afrah turned white at the sight before him: the messenger of the mighty Araad was lying dead on the palace floor!

"This is a disaster!" said Sacardion to Prince Afrah. "We must capture Saadoun at any cost and hand him over to King Araad."

Prince Afrah ordered all his men, together with the men who had come with the messenger Darbal, to seize Saadoun at any cost. But Saadoun's warriors had been waiting for their leader outside the walls of the city of Dour. A fight to the death now started between Saadoun's small group of men and the hundreds of soldiers that Prince Afrah had sent against them.

Saadoun, seeing that they were greatly outnumbered, called to his men that they were free to leave, for he did not wish to force anyone to fight a hopeless battle because of him. But with one voice his men answered that they would fight beside him whatever happened.

"Victory or death!" they shouted.

The battle was long and hard, and many on both sides met their deaths. Saadoun, his shield red with his enemy's blood and his body covered with wounds, felt his arms grow heavy from the long fight. How long could he and his few men continue to fight against so many? Then, from a distance, he saw a horseman approaching in a cloud of dust. Immediately, the horseman charged at Prince Afrah's men, striking out with his sword. The man was like a savage wolf among a flock of sheep.

Saadoun rode his horse up to the other horseman. "Who are you, noble warrior, who has come to help us with our fight?"

"Do you not recognise me, friend Saadoun?" - and the warrior lifted the veil that covered the lower part of his face. It was Desert Fox.

The battle continued fiercely, but when Prince Afrah heard that Desert Fox had arrived and was fighting beside his friend Saadoun, he ordered his men to stop fighting.

Though he had agreed to the wicked Sacardion's advice and had promised that his daughter could marry King Araad, Prince Afrah was happy to see that Desert Fox had returned safely.

"Welcome back, my son," Prince Afrah said to him.

"Why are your men fighting my friend Saadoun?" Desert Fox asked the ruler of Dour. Prince Afrah then told him about King Araad having sent Darbal as his messenger to ask for the hand of Shama.

"You were away for so long," said Prince Afrah, "that we all thought you would not return to marry Shama."

"And what answer did you give to this man Darbal?" asked Desert Fox. Prince Afrah was embarrassed by the question.

"Ask your friend Saadoun," he said. "In fact, no reply has been given to King Araad, for Saadoun killed Darbal in a fight."

"Is this why you were fighting Saadoun?" asked Desert Fox.

"King Araad is a powerful ruler," Prince Afrah reminded Desert Fox, "and his messengers cannot be killed without someone paying the price."

"Saadoun is my friend," said Desert Fox, "and while I am alive I shall always be there to help him. As for your daughter, she will be the wife of no-one but me, for here is the Book of the Nile which you asked for."

That evening a great party was held in the palace of Dour, with Desert Fox sitting at the right hand of Prince Afrah and Saadoun at the left. It was a party to celebrate the coming marriage of Desert Fox with Shama. While they were at the table, Desert Fox told Prince Afrah and Saadoun about his adventures: how he had been imprisoned in the pit and how he had been given a magic cap that made him invisible and which had made it possible for him to take the Book of the Nile.

Sacardion was in another part of the palace. He was thinking evil thoughts about the death of Darbal and how Saadoun must be captured and made to pay the price. Most of all he feared having to tell King Araad that he would no longer be able to marry Shama. Was there still time to stop her marriage to Desert Fox? Only, he decided, if he could arrange to have Desert Fox killed.

Chapter Six

King Araad was sitting in his palace when a messenger entered and told him that some soldiers were waiting to see him.

"What soldiers?" he demanded.

"Some of the men of Darbal whom you sent to Prince Afrah," answered the messenger.

King Araad was furious when he learned that Darbal had been killed in Prince Afrah's palace. But more than anything else, he was full of anger at the news that Desert Fox - now known to be Seif bin Ziyazan, son of the former King of Yemen - had returned and planned to marry Shama.

While the king sat thinking about what action he should take against the three men - Saadoun, Prince Afrah and Desert Fox - his minister Sacardion entered. Sacardion had come at great speed from the court of Prince Afrah: it was necessary for him to speak to King Araad urgently.

"Your Majesty, I have thought much about the serious position we face. It is clear that Desert Fox must die as soon as possible. If he becomes ruler of the Red City in place of his mother, it would be a disaster for us."

"Why do you say that, Sacardion?" asked King Araad.

"Because the armies of the Red City are already strong and would become much more powerful under Desert Fox. I advise Your Majesty that we Ethiopians must first move against Queen Kamariyya," insisted Sacardion.

"But what about Saadoun, who killed our messenger Darbal?" asked King Araad. "Should we not punish him for what he did?"

"I agree with Your Majesty, but in my opinion this Seif bin Ziyazan is the real danger to us. First of all, though, we must crush the armies of Queen Kamariyya."

King Araad agreed with his minister's advice and sent a message to Prince Afrah ordering him to advance against Queen Kamariyya and the Red City. He also wrote a letter to Queen Kamariyya herself, saying: "We, King Araad and our ally Prince Afrah, are determined to conquer the Red City. If you surrender to us we shall spare the city and allow you to continue as its queen. If not, you and its people will be put to death."

But Queen Kamariyya, as Sacardion had known, was a proud woman. She therefore replied to King Araad's letter by saying that she was ready to defend her city against any attack. She immediately began to strengthen the walls of the Red City and brought in supplies of food from neighbouring countries. Her spies told her that the armies of Prince Afrah, including Desert Fox and Saadoun, were advancing towards the Red City.

When, several days later, the armies were camped outside the city walls, Kamariyya left the city at night, secretly and in disguise, and went to the tent where Desert Fox was about to go to sleep. Prince Afrah planned to attack the city the next morning.

Desert Fox was surprised to be visited at such a late hour by this woman. He did not of course know that she was his real mother. It was only later, when they talked about the battle that was to take place, that she told him the truth about his birth and that he was her son. Pretending to feel for him the same love that every mother feels for her child, she kissed the top of his head while tears filled her eyes.

"Yes," she told him, "you are my son, Seif bin Ziyazan. This Red City is yours and was previously ruled by your father, who was a mighty king. Return to your city, my son, and rule it again as your father would wish."

Seif bin Ziyazan was amazed at her words. "How do I know that you are telling me the truth?" he asked.

"Later tonight," she told him, "I shall bring some men who knew your father well and were at his court when you were still a baby. They will recognise you as his son and then you can be sure about the truth of what I have told you." Kamariyya then wrapped herself in her cloak and left the tent as secretly as she had entered.

Desert Fox sat alone thinking about this new event in his life. He remembered what Sheikh Abdul Salam had told him about himself and that he was really Seif bin Ziyazan, the son of the King of Yemen.

Some time later, Kamariyya returned to the tent. This time she brought four men from the palace, all old men who had known Seif's father. She had explained to them that she had at last found her son and that he was one of the commanders of the armies that were now preparing to attack the city.

As soon as the four men saw Desert Fox they knew that he was Seif, son of the former King of the Red City, and they bowed down in front of him and kissed the ground at his feet.

"Welcome, Master," said the eldest of them. "You are exactly as your father was at your age."

"And the birthmark on your cheek - we saw it the very first day you were shown to us by your mother."

"You are without doubt the son of Kamariyya," said another, "and this is your city. Welcome to your city and be our ruler, for this is what your father wanted."

Desert Fox was amazed at what he was hearing, while his mother told him how glad she was to have found him at last and that he would soon be the ruler of the Red City. Desert Fox believed everything she told him and was filled with warmth for his mother who had suddenly entered his life.

"I shall go now, my son," she told him, "and I shall tell the people that I have found my son and that it is he who will rule over them in future."

She also took him to one side and whispered to him that his father had left a great treasure and that it was buried in a secret place.

CHAPTER SEVEN

Kamariyya left Seif and went back to the Red City with the four men. It was now late at night and they agreed that early the next morning they would announce to the people of the city the good news about Seif.

"But first," she told the four men, "let us celebrate this wonderful news. I shall tell my maid-servant to bring us food and drink."

Kamariyya went out of the room to tell her servant to prepare delicious food for her and the four men. But before she gave them the food, she added some deadly poison. The four men ate and drank. Within minutes all four were lying dead.

Kamariyya ordered the maidservant to help her throw the bodies into an old well. When this was done, Kamariyya stabbed the maidservant and threw her body into the well too.

Early the next morning Kamariyya left the city on her horse and rode back to her son's tent. Just before dawn she and Seif bin Ziyazan rode together into the desert. She told him that she would take him to where his father's treasure was hidden so that he might enjoy the riches and be generous to the people of the Red City. After many hours of hard riding, they came to a shady tree growing beside a small water-hole.

"We have arrived, my son," she told him, and the two of them got off their horses.

Seif went to the edge of the water-hole. As he bent over to drink some water, Kamariyya crept up behind him and struck him with her sword. But

at the last moment he moved his head and the sword went through his cloak instead. Immediately she struck again, this time cutting into the flesh of his shoulder. Again and again she struck at Seif while he tried to defend himself with his arm. Blood flowed from his wounds as he tried to escape from her. Then he fell to the ground and lost consciousness.

Thinking that he was dead, Kamariyya went and untied her horse. Several hours later she was back in the Red City.

It was morning before Seif opened his eyes to the sun's burning rays. His whole body ached and he was unable to move at all. He cried out in pain from the wounds and asked God to allow him to die quickly. As the sun rose in the sky, its heat beat more and more heavily upon him. Still half-conscious, he heard the sound of birds in the branches of the tree above him. Quite clearly he heard one bird say to another: "Peace be upon you." And, quite clearly, he heard the other bird reply: "And upon you be peace and the mercy of God and His blessings."

Then the first bird said: "Who could imagine a mother would behave to her child like this!"

"This is not the first time she has tried to kill him," replied the other bird.

Seif was amazed at the two birds talking to each other in human voices. In fact, he felt he recognised the two voices. Then he realised that these were the voices of Sheikh Abdul Salam and Sheikh Jiyad, the two holy sheikhs he had met during his travels.

Then one of the birds said that the medicine for Seif's wounds lay close by. All Seif had to do, it said, was to take some of the leaves of the tree under which he was lying, to chew them and then to put them on his wounds. But how could he reach the leaves when he could not move at all? Then a great wind began to blow and some of the leaves fell down beside him. He collected them and put them in his mouth and then onto his many wounds. The pain immediately left his body and the wounds began to heal. Soon he was strong enough to stand. To his relief, he saw that his horse was nearby and he thanked God for giving him a way to escape.

Seif bin Ziyazan - or Desert Fox as he had been known until now - travelled for many days and nights through stony deserts. He drank from the wells that he found and ate from the plants that he knew were not poisonous. Then, in the far distance, he saw two high mountains. The one on the right was white-coloured, and the one on the left was brown-coloured, while between them lay the deep blue waters of a sea. He rode towards the brown-coloured mountain. As he came near, he saw that on its top was a house built of white stone. Rising from the middle of the house into the sky was a great column. When he reached the house he called out: "Peace be upon those who live in this house."

A deep voice answered from inside: "Welcome to you, O Seif bin Ziyazan."

"How did you know my name?" asked Seif in amazement.

Then an old man with a long white moustache came out of the house. "I have been waiting for you for twenty years," said the man. "Come inside and rest and have some food."

Seif entered the beautifully furnished house, with fine carpets on the floors. He was surprised to find that the food was ready, laid out on a brass tray. The man sat down with him and Seif ate with the pleasure of someone who has not eaten properly for many days. While Seif ate, the man told him that he was in charge of the treasures that had been waiting for him.

"They are the treasures of your grandfather," explained the man, "and you have now inherited them."

"And may I ask your name?" said Seif.

"My name," said the man, "is Ikhmim the Scholar. Tonight you must rest and in the morning we shall go together to collect the treasures."

Seif slept well and in the morning Ikhmim the Scholar led him to the pillar that rose up in the middle of the house. Seif saw strange writings on the pillar: magical inscriptions with secret messages. He asked about these and Ikhmim the Scholar answered: "I have spent my life studying them, but I am still unable to read some of these writings. They describe the secrets of the world but only those who can read them may know their meanings."

"Could you teach me some of what you have learned?" Seif asked him.

Ikhmim the Scholar shook his head with a smile. "Each must make the effort to learn for himself - nothing may be passed on."

Seif looked up at the towering pillar and asked: "And what am I to do?"

"Look at the pillar and see if you can climb up it."

"That is easy," said Seif, "for there are steps cut into the pillar. They seem to go to the top."

"Only you can see these steps," said Ikhmim the Scholar, "which means that only you have the right to climb to the top."

Seif started to climb and when he had reached the top of the pillar, he called down: "And now what shall I do?"

"What do you see in front of you?"

"Two marks, like footprints in the sand."

"Place your feet on them," said Ikhmim. Seif's feet fitted exactly on the footprints.

"Now be brave and throw yourself from the pillar," said Ikhmim.

Closing his eyes, Seif did as he was told and found himself at the top of another pillar on the mountain opposite, with a wonderful palace facing him. Ikhmim told him to go and knock at the door of the palace and to give his full name when he was asked.

"There are two treasures that you must collect from inside the palace," he told Seif. "In the far room you will find an old man lying on a bed. On his chest you will see a plate of solid gold with a silver chain. Ask his permission, then take it from him and return to me. You must then go back to the palace and at the end of the old man's bed you will find a sword in its sheath. But, whatever happens, do not take the sword out of its sheath. Say to the man: 'O king, permit me to take this sword and to fight with it for the sake of God.'"

Seif did exactly as he was told. When he went inside the second time he asked the old man if he might have the sword, and the man pointed to it with his right hand. Seif picked it up but as he was walking away he became curious: why should he not take it out of its sheath and look at it quickly? As he pulled the sword out, Seif felt the earth tremble beneath his feet and a terrifying scream filled the air, while a great wind blew through the palace.

The next moment, Seif found himself lying outside the palace walls. Ikhmim was sitting by his head and waiting for him to open his eyes.

"What happened?" asked Seif.

"Did I not warn you not to take the sword out of its sheath?" said Ikhmim.

Suddenly Ikhmim disappeared. Seif noticed that he no longer had the magic sword: he had lost it as the price of his curiosity. Alone now, Seif looked around him and found that the palace was completely surrounded by water. His only way of return was somehow to reach the other pillar from which he had jumped. He therefore climbed up the pillar above him and, with fear in his heart, threw himself off it. But this time he was not protected by the blessing of Ikhmim the Scholar and he fell straight down into the waters below. He felt himself rushing through them at great speed, and then, with no more breath left in his body, all went black.

CHAPTER EIGHT

Unable to breathe, Seif bin Ziyazan felt certain that he would meet his death in these deep waters. But when he next opened his eyes he found himself lying on the sandy shore of a great sea. Half of him was still in the water and he could feel its coolness against his legs.

A large tree grew at the water's edge. He walked to it and took off his clothes and hung them on the branches to dry. After that, he looked around for something to eat, but there was nothing except for some small, yellow fruit growing on desert bushes. Because he was so hungry, he tried them but found them bitter and feared that they might be poisonous.

When his clothes were dry he put them on. From far off he saw a cloud of dust approaching. He knew that this must be a group of horsemen coming in his direction, so he quickly climbed into the leafy tree to hide.

As he watched the cloud of dust, it approached closer and closer. The man in command got off his horse and came to sit in the shade of the tree.

"Search for him through the whole valley," he told his men, and they rode off in different directions. One of the men stayed to make a fire and began cooking some food. Seif, whose stomach was empty, sat in the top branches of the tree as the smell of the meat rose up to him. When the man in command had finished his meal, he lay down and went to sleep.

Before sunset the other soldiers returned and reported that they had searched everywhere but found no-one. They then sat down and began preparing food for their evening meal. Once again, Seif was filled with the pains of hunger at the sight and smell of the food.

Soon the soldiers had eaten and were deeply asleep, but no sleep came to Seif as he sat uncomfortably in the tree with his stomach aching for food and water. When morning came at last, the men sat down to a large breakfast with glasses of steaming tea. Seif could no longer stop himself. Without realising what he was doing, he called out: "Men, I am a stranger and I am in need of food." He immediately regretted what he had done, but it was too late.

"Come down," ordered the man in command. Seif climbed down and was immediately surrounded by the soldiers, with their swords ready. As for Seif, he had no sword or other weapon to defend himself with.

"Who are you?" asked the man. "And what are you doing here?"

"Let me eat first," begged Seif, "before I answer your questions."

"Eat as much as you want and then we shall see whether you are the person we are looking for."

When he had eaten enough, Seif prepared himself to answer their questions.

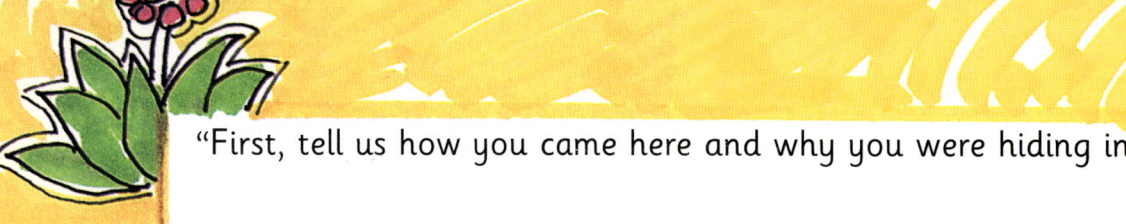

"First, tell us how you came here and why you were hiding in this tree."

Seif decided to make up a long story from his head: "I was a merchant travelling with all my goods on a boat. There was a terrible storm and the boat was wrecked. I was washed up on an island. I did not know how to escape; then one day a great bird landed on the island and I tied myself to one of its legs and it flew off with me. While it was flying, it began pecking at me with its enormous beak. I fell and again found myself in the sea. I swam till I came to this shore and climbed up this tree."

The man in command laughed and shook his head. "Do you believe a word of this story?" he asked his men. They all laughed and said they did not.

"I think you are the person we were sent to look for," said the man in charge. While he was speaking, a horseman rode up to them and got off his horse. It was an elderly man clothed all in white, whom Seif immediately recognised as Ikhmim the Scholar.

"Yes, this is the man," said Ikhmim. "This is Seif bin Ziyazan."

On hearing this name the commander and his men bowed in front of Seif.

"You have done well to find him," said Ikhmim the Scholar to the commander. "You and your men will be well rewarded. Now you may leave us."

When they were alone, Ikhmim took out the gold jar from inside his cloak and said: "I wanted to find you to give you this and to show you its secret."

The old man placed the jar in Seif's hands and rubbed it gently.

Suddenly Seif heard a deep voice saying: "At your service, O wise man of the age."

A small figure, the size of a young boy but with the face of an old man, appeared before them. "I am Airoud," said the figure. "I am the servant of the jar." His bright eyes looked at Seif.

"Do you know who I am?" Seif asked him.

"You are King Seif bin Ziyazan," answered Airoud. "In your name this jar has been kept all these years. Now at last you have received it and I shall serve you as you wish."

CHAPTER NINE

After saying goodbye to Ikhmim the Scholar, Seif gave his first command to Airoud, the servant of the jar.

"Take me to the Red City, which is ruled by Queen Kamariyya."

At the walls of the city, Seif could no longer see the tents of Prince Afrah and Saadoun the Black. He feared that perhaps they had been defeated in battle by Kamariyya's soldiers. He therefore decided to hide in the mountains that surrounded the city and to wait until he found out what had happened to Saadoun and Prince Afrah before trying to enter the city.

Soon he saw two horsemen riding along one of the rocky mountain paths. When they came near, they bowed down to Seif.

"Where are you from?" he asked them.

"We are from the army of Saadoun the Black," replied one of the men.

"Where is he?" asked Seif impatiently. "Take me to him immediately!"

"That is not possible," said the second man. "Our leader Saadoun has been taken prisoner and is being held in the city of Dour."

"How is that?" asked Seif.

"He was taken by King Araad's men; King Araad himself has moved to the city of Dour in preparation for his marriage to Shama."

Seif instructed the two men to return to their companions. 'I shall join you as soon as I can," he told them.

As soon as they had gone, Seif rubbed the golden jar and the servant Airoud appeared before him.

"Take me to the city of Dour," he ordered.

As he approached the city, Seif heard the sound of pipes and drums and voices singing.

"Leave me on a mountain while you go into the city and find out what is happening," Seif ordered Airoud.

Airoud was soon back to tell his master that the noise of music was in preparation for a wedding feast. Shama was to be married to the great King Araad.

"A tent has been prepared for the bride," Airoud told Seif.

"Take me to the tent," said Seif, "and watch what happens from a distance. If you see that I am in any danger, bring me and Shama straight to this mountain."

Seif approached the tent cautiously. He stood for a while outside it and listened to the crying from inside: it was Shama repeating his name. Seif entered the tent without her noticing.

"Shama," he whispered to her. It was as if she had seen a ghost, for she had been told that Seif was dead and that she would never see him again. She fell at his feet, weeping with joy.

They told each other what had happened since they had last been together. She told him how Kamariyya, his mother, had said her son had been killed by bandits in the desert. The wicked queen had also sent men to capture Saadoun and they had taken him to Prince Afrah who had thrown him into his prison in Dour. As soon as Sacardion had heard that Seif was dead he had persuaded Prince Afrah to let King Araad marry his daughter Shama.

While Seif and Shama were talking, her father, Prince Afrah, entered the tent in order to take her to the wedding ceremony. He stared at Seif in amazement, unable to speak. Seif went up to him angrily.

"Did you not promise me your daughter in marriage?" he demanded.

"Your mother told us you were dead," said the Prince weakly.

"If you were not Shama's father, I would cut you in two with this sword," Seif told him. Prince Afrah ran from the tent and went back to the city of Dour to tell King Araad that Seif was alive.

As soon as King Araad heard the news, he ordered his soldiers to surround the tent and to allow no-one to escape from it. But Airoud, who had been watching everything, came and carried Seif and Shama away to the mountain. There, a tent had been set up and the most delicious food had been prepared to celebrate the two lovers being together again.

The wicked Sacardion was mad with anger when he heard that Seif had not died in the desert. When messengers told him that Seif and Shama had gone to the nearby mountain, he made his way there with several men. He met Seif and explained that both he and King Araad had been promised the hand of Shama in marriage.

"You should not blame Prince Afrah," Sacardion said with a dark smile, "for he was told by your own mother that you had died in the desert. That is why he gave his daughter in marriage to another man. And since no woman can be a wife to two men, there is only one way in which this matter can be settled."

"How is that?" asked Seif.

"By man-to-man combat," answered Sacardion. "But King Araad is now an old man and you are still young, so it would not be fair for you to fight each other. Therefore, King Araad must be allowed to choose someone to fight on his behalf."

Sacardion looked at Seif. "Do you agree to that?" he asked.

"Let him choose whoever he wishes," answered Seif. "I am ready to fight anyone for the right to marry Shama."

"Make yourself ready for battle tomorrow morning," said Sacardion and returned to the City of Dour. He was smiling to himself, for already a plan had formed in his mind which he felt would put an end to Seif bin Ziyazan.

After this, Sacardion went straight to tell King Araad of the bargain he had made with Seif bin Ziyazan.

"But there is no-one who is able to compete against Seif in man-to-man combat," said King Araad. "Who among all our men could we send to challenge him?"

"Among the Ethiopians there is no-one," admitted Sacardion. "Yet there is one man - and only one - who is capable of defeating Seif bin Ziyazan in man-to-man combat."

"And who is that?" asked King Araad.

"Saadoun the Black," said Sacardion.

"But Saadoun would never fight against his friend Seif," objected the King.

Sacardion gave a wicked smile. "Only if it were a matter of life and death - his own life."

"What do you mean?"

"Saadoun was tricked by Queen Kamariyya and handed over to Prince Afrah. Saadoun now lies in the prisons of this palace. Offer him his freedom if he fights against Seif and kills him. At the same time tell him that he will be put to death if he refuses. There is no man who would not accept such an offer."

"You are right, Sacardion," said the King. "And if Seif wins?"

"Whatever the result of the fight," Sacardion pointed out, "it will be terrible for Seif: he is either killed or he kills his best friend."

"Sacardion," said King Araad, "your idea is devilish and brilliant!"

Saadoun was brought up from the prisons, his hands and feet in chains.

"Saadoun, this is your last chance," the King told him. "Tomorrow you will be taken to the main square where your head will be cut off and displayed on the city walls as a warning to all traitors. But we offer you one chance to save your life."

"What do you want from me?" asked Saadoun.

"Tomorrow," explained Sacardion, "a warrior is to be chosen to meet one of our enemies in man-to-man combat. King Araad and I know that you are the only warrior who is able to defeat him."

"I am ready to meet anyone in man-to-man combat," answered Saadoun, "if it will save my life. Who is the man I must fight?"

"It is none other than your friend Seif bin Ziyazan," said the King. "Are you still willing to fight?"

"Seif?" asked Saadoun. "So Seif is not dead?" Only with difficulty was Saadoun able to hide his joy at the news.

"It is your only chance, Saadoun," the King reminded him. "Either your head or the head of Seif bin Ziyazan will be stuck on the city walls tomorrow. It is your choice."

"It is true that he used to be a good friend of mine," admitted Saadoun, "but life is sweet and death is bitter. Tomorrow I agree to fight him."

King Araad ordered that the chains be taken off Saadoun's hands and feet and that he be allowed to spend the night in one of the rooms of the palace.

The next morning Saadoun, riding a fine horse and with a shining sword in his hand, came out from the Ethiopian army to face Seif bin Ziyazan in battle. On his head he wore a helmet with long ostrich feathers, while the lower part of his face was covered with a veil. He could not be recognised and only King Araad and Sacardion knew that it was Saadoun.

Seif rode down from the mountain on his favourite horse, a powerful black stallion. His helmet was decorated with black raven's feathers. In his left hand he carried a heavy shield made of leather and in his right hand the sword with which he had won many battles. Then, with a wild shout, Saadoun gave a kick and his horse raced towards the approaching figure

of Seif. The sound of the horses' hooves and the clash of swords broke the silence. Several times the two men charged, exchanging blows as they passed each other, then turning for a further charge.

Suddenly, a great cry of astonishment came from the soldiers watching the battle as Saadoun, instead of striking at Seif as he passed, jumped from his horse. He ran across to Seif, knelt down and lifted his veil.

"King Seif, I am Saadoun," he called out to him.

"I thought I knew that special way you have with a sword," Seif said to him. "Quickly mount your horse, my friend, for these Ethiopians will soon be after us."

Before the soldiers could get to their horses, Seif and Saadoun easily escaped and rode back to their hide-out in the mountains.

CHAPTER TEN

Shama had been watching the battle from the top of the mountain that overlooked the city of Dour. She hurried towards Seif as he got down from his horse, delighted at his safe return with his friend.

Saadoun told Seif how he had been tricked by Queen Kamariyya, who had sent a message to him saying that his friend Seif was in danger and needed his help. Kamariyya's men had then ambushed Saadoun when he had gone out to the place where Kamariyya had said Seif was. After that he had been taken to Prince Afrah's prison in the city of Dour.

"I fear for you, Seif, from her," said Shama.

"We should go to the Red City," suggested Saadoun, "and break the power of your mother, Queen Kamariyya."

Seif rubbed the magic plate and Airoud appeared in front of them. "Take us to the Red City," commanded Seif and in seconds the three of them found themselves in front of the tall red walls of the city.

Meanwhile, outside the walls of the city, the mighty army that Prince Afrah had agreed to send against Queen Kamariyya was encamped. With them were the men of Saadoun the Black, who were overjoyed to have their leader safely back with them. The army then attacked the city's walls and a fierce battle started. But the people of the Red City had suffered under the rule of Kamariyya and were no longer prepared to give their lives to defend her. The rumour had spread that Seif bin Ziyazan, the son of the former king, had appeared in the land and many people were saying that he should be made king in place of his mother.

Kamariyya saw that her army was beaten and that her enemies were climbing the walls of the city. Quickly she ordered that the city gates be opened to Seif and the army of Prince Afrah, for she saw that her only hope was to pretend to welcome her son to the city.

In the meantime, King Araad, King of the Ethiopians, was full of rage that both Seif and Saadoun were still alive.

"All your plans have failed," he shouted at Sacardion. "Seif bin Ziyazan has escaped unharmed from the battle. We had Saadoun in our prison here at the palace, and at your suggestion he was set free so that he might kill Seif. Where are they both now? Where, too, is Shama who was to become my wife?"

Sacardion was both wicked and clever and always blamed someone else for anything that went wrong.

"O mighty King," he answered, "that traitor Prince Afrah is responsible for all these disasters. You should take revenge on him, for he always planned to marry Shama to that enemy of ours, the Yemeni Seif bin Ziyazan."

King Araad ordered that Prince Afrah should be brought to him in chains. He also called for the court executioner.

"Your time has come, treacherous dog," King Araad told Prince Afrah, who tried to beg for his life. Two guards took hold of Prince Afrah and threw him to the ground in front of the executioner.

When Seif was met at the gate of the city by his mother, Queen Kamariyya, he told his guards to lock her in her rooms. He then entered the city with Saadoun and Shama on either side of him. The citizens cheered as he passed among them.

"Welcome to your city, King Seif bin Ziyazan!" they shouted.

The first thing Seif did when he entered the Red City was to empty the prisons of all the people that Queen Kamariyya had thrown into them. He declared a public holiday of seven days and distributed gifts to the poor in preparation for his wedding to Shama. Then, seated in the palace, he turned a sad face to his friend Saadoun.

"And now," he said, "before we give our attention to my marriage, let me decide my mother's fate."

"She must be put to death," said Saadoun, "for the evil that she has done in the past and so that she may never again harm anyone."

"But what man can order the death of his own mother?" said Seif. "That is something I cannot do."

At that moment one of the palace men entered to tell Seif that Queen Kamariyya was dead.

"How?" asked Seif, and despite himself his eyes filled with tears. The man said that one of the maidservants had stabbed her to death.

"May God have mercy upon her," said Seif bin Ziyazan. Then he turned to Shama. "Our days of happiness together will begin tonight with our marriage."

"But how can we marry when my father is not here?" asked Shama. So Seif rubbed the magic plate and ordered Airoud to bring Prince Afrah to the Red City.

Airoud arrived just in time to save him from the executioner. Prince Afrah, on his arrival, embraced his daughter tenderly. Then he turned to Seif. "I owe you my life. Forgive me for any wrongs I have done to you in the past. Now, by giving you my beloved daughter as your wife, you will become even more of a son to me."

That night the people of the Red City feasted long into the night in celebration of the wedding of their new king. And, as was told in the ancient books, there now began a time of prosperity, freedom and happiness.